THE GAR...
ONKEL ARNOLD

The Gardens of Onkel Arnold

DAVID JACOBS

PETERLOO POETS

First published in 2004
by Peterloo Poets
The Old Chapel, Sand Lane, Calstock, Cornwall PL18 9QX, U.K.

**A catalogue record for this book is available
from the British Library**

ISBN   1-904324-22-3

Printed in Great Britain by
Antony Rowe Ltd, Chippenham, Wilts.

ACKNOWLEDGEMENTS

Acknowledgements are due to the editors of the following journals in which some of these poems first appeared: *Accountancy Age, Ambit, Contemporary Review, Envoi, Fiddlehead* (Canada), *The Haiku Quarterly, The Honest Ulsterman, The Iron Book of British Haiku, London Magazine, Oxford Poetry, PEN, PEN International, Poetry Postcard Quarterly, Poetry Wales, Redoubt* (Australia), *Spokes, Stand, Tandem, Tees Valley Writer.*

Contents

SPORT, LOVE AND MISCELLANEOUS

FATHERHOOD

THE GARDENS OF ONKEL ARNOLD

The Old Lily Pond

The water mopes inside its sunken shrine,
The tiled rim, diminished
By decades and purged
Of brightness. Now the stone
Maintains a calm, dank dignity
Around the darkened pool.

The earth won't let it go now.
Every year it hugs the unresistant stone
More closely, keeping it
From simple excavation and the might
Of winds. In one corner,
Dismal lilies float.

Peonies

Marauding ants make their pregnancies
Unbeautiful, dragging their
Menacing slicks across the unborn.

Their claret blooms become too large
And gregarious. Within days, the high stalks
Dip their fishing rods. The petals

Fall and scatter into pools of blood.
I wish them to be upright,
Smart survivors, lingering with

The marigold and rose who stray
Devoutly into equinox.
Their failures disappoint, but when

Their brittle straw lies down
Across the path, I think
To let them carry on and not

To make those wild and thinning
Scalps of women leap into
The light. Next time I shall expect

Much less of them, relish instead
Their fearless rampaging,
Boisterous brevity, crimson gold.

The Gardens of Onkel Arnold

He leaves them only for meal-times and God,
His eightieth birthday not a time for taking stock
Or dealing with the consternation
Of his children. Onkel Arnold, Onkel Arnold,
They call from their different heights.
Who will nurture us when you are gone?

But Onkel Arnold hacks away with his flashing
Moon blade. Spotting him inside his world-sized acreage
Is like a game – is that rustling a bird
Or fox? Then you see him, high astride
The mighty cliffs, re-pointing on a step
Too narrow even for a child's truck.

Perhaps he's as secure there as an eagle
Standing by a nest of babes, its talons
Marrying surely with the granite ledge.
Or perhaps he doesn't care, when getting down
In safety takes him to the wife he doesn't
Speak to any more, and falling brings him to God.

Never Mind

Never mind that the Bonsai tree
Your colleagues gave you
As a parting gift
Is dying.
Next to it on the windowsill
The hyancinths are flowering fast
And giving off
A glorious blue scent.

Grass Cutting

In bullfrog pose I slice at tufted crowns,
Turning on mischief makers, stragglers,
The quiet, furtive types.
The shears' arthritic joints
Drives freshness out.
I work too quickly.
This is how I write poems,
Demanding, early, the impossible
Resplendent lawns
Devoid of bumpiness.

Snapping at shrubbery hurts less.
The violence is more fun,
The results less peripheral.
Days later, blades become portcullises
Of straw, but in the beds
New homes occur for space
And nothingness, new
Routes for air and light.
I tidy the dead,
Scooping with ungloved hands.

Conifer

Like thoughts we place not idly
Inside each other and leave to come true,

So we have entrusted to the winter
This wounded conifer of ours. Novice

Gardeners, we rely on luck and faith.
First welded to the soil it stood

As noble as a penguin, fully breasted,
Till a brown and jagged cutlass ate

Into its heart. I strummed the foliage,
Watched it silently vibrate. Indoors

We cannot see the wound and wonder
If the healing has begun out of its

Medicine of air and solitude. It ducks
Before the wind like a souwestered

Crewman cowers against the storm.
We wait by calm and windless lamps

Until we venture out in kinder air
To what came true, in our absented care.

Snow Melting

The pond stays frozen shut.
Mother-of-pearl amongst
The shampooed shrubbery.

The Cherry Tree

You arrived, and in a curious kind of way,
I arrived also. Before, you were simply an idea, unpatented,
Beautiful as a ball of mist inside my brain.

Yesterday, you planted a cherry tree. I watched you
From the window, forking the earth, alive as a child.
In the morning, while you were still asleep,

I drew back the curtain. A gauntlet of white blossom
Glinted in the sun. I felt happy, but my heart turned
Like a planet. I wept for the beauties of mist.

PEOPLE AND PLACES

The Mountbatten Festival of Music

(for Gerald Bowthorpe)

My dear Gerald, thank you for inviting us
To share your box in the Royal Albert Hall.
The Lord Mountbatten Festival of Music, the fourth
Year running we've been your guests, or is it
The fifth? We admit we were sceptics
To begin with – all that military razzmatazz,
Helmeted marines marching from nowhere
Into the auditorium, drumming in unison.
And the audience with their stripes and medals
Stamping their feet and clapping them home,
Not for us, we thought, too low brow,
(Despite a touch of Elgar), but now we're smitten,
Rejoicing in patriotism and song, and hope
Our names will never be deleted from your list.
You and Didi host the occasion admirably,
Keep our glasses filled, the eats continually
On the move. We like your other guests,
Nothing fancy. We enjoy their chat
Before it all begins. Waiting for the lights
We scan the hall and marvel in its cornice work
And all those fairy tale acoustic clouds.
Our voices may not be particularly good,
But when we reach 'We'll meet again' and 'The
White Cliffs of Dover', we intend to let rip.

An Old Friend

Yesterday, while you were still in Frankfurt,
I met up with an old friend.
He arrived as I was watching TV and comparing
Our new carpet to a tranquil blue sea.

He settled down, gently, inside my head
Like a small and joyous ball of mist,
Circulating just enough to fill up
The hollows, the crevasses, the intricate dark places.

We chatted quite a lot to begin with,
About the olden days and, later, about you.
I noticed how, in the manner of Dorian Gray,
He seemed, hardly, to have aged.

On the tube I suggested we all met,
And suddenly I felt him leaking
Slowly out of me, and the re-assertion
Of familiar trees shedding their ghosthood.

In the end I was relieved he'd gone, as you'll be
When you return to find me still here
And much the same as when you left me –
Like this solid and loyal old house of ours

(A good bit tidier than when you went!)
And me slouching inside it,
Overwrought about my job and complaining
Over a small swab of tightness inside my chest.

The Café by the Water

The man-made lagoon sparkles like a brochure.
Moored, luxurious craft line up at roll call,
High masts, Christian at the top, ropes
An alien geometry that drop their wigwams
On to stripped and spotless decks. On the bows
Princess whoever is the favoured name.

Along smart walkways, groomed, superior shops
Blaze fruit and flowers, ornaments and souvenirs.
One offers mohair, tartan skirts and scarves,
Another, all things nautical – seascapes
Lushly framed, and ships' brass style instruments,
Flossed and polished to exacting gleams.

In the café by the water, Leonardo tells us how
He makes his money not on quiche but salads,
Cheerfully insisting that the sums work out.
Who cares, as long as he survives and customers
Can keep their view across the water
To the gabled Charles Dickens pub and restaurant.

The Cleaner's Tale

WORK

He arrives at five
To polish the banisters,
Lays out cloths

Like a bazaar,
Puts a plastic bucket
On the landing.

He rubs on Brasso,
Working at his own pace.
He doesn't whistle

Or hum. He listens
To the views
Of the security guard.

LEISURE

Sometimes he occupies
A bench, beneath
Tall trees, legs

Crossed like a swastika,
An arm along
The back enclosing

Nobody. Mostly, he
Wanders among
The terraces,

Moving stiffly,
Not venturing
Into pubs or shops.

BUCKET

Mostly it just
Sits dumbly
On the landing –

The colour
Of belisha beacons,
The inside

Stained like
Gunshot wounds.
As hours pass

Cloths and rags
Get draped
Across its rim.

BANNISTERS

Uncarpeted stairs,
Musty cabinets
On the landings.

From the windows,
Rooftop views
Over West London.

The golden river
Flows down
Every flight,

Sweeps around
Bends, gets
Locked up at night.

Lifestyle

FLAT

Shelves in an alcove, a few books,
Lighting, not dim nor over-bright.
TV and deck. Plants numbered right.

Saloon style doors that opened to
A length of streamlined kitchen, smooth
As coffins, polished up for use.

The bedroom: not much else apart
From dressing table, double bed,
Erotica, in slabs of art.

PHASE

Once, she remarked, it was a phase,
As if accepting how it was.
First dates got labelled 'My new man',

And she would urge 'I'm really keen',
Or 'Things are getting hot'; each phrase
Seemed almost a demand for praise.

Her tennis club, a kind of scene,
Going to discos in a crowd,
Dancing till late, the music loud.

ETIQUETTE

A stack of postcards in her flat,
A table where she sometimes sat
And wrote out thanks for this or that.

A pot she always kept for tea,
A proper brew, strict she could be
That mats were used, but quietly.

Going for walks – a friend to stay –
Across the park at close of play,
The action, never far away.

A Woman Observed

A strange concoction, this ample room of yours.
The painted floorboards' sweep of universe,
The simple table and the lamp, a misty cabinet

Fits barely half the alcove. Yet an original
Exists inside a timber frame, a gold edged
Mirror hangs. You sit before a buzzing screen

Continuing the excellent beginning to your life –
The director of a publishing (world
Famous) house, your tennis has improved

By leaps and bounds, and you pursue a part time
MBA with grisly passion, late into the night,
Filling your head with complex formulae.

In time I think you will become your own
Magnificent creation – a high priestess
Or woman of the hunt, sensuous and supreme

Upon the saddle, speeding between the trees,
With hair that tracks the contours of the wind.
You long to travel to the world's most

Lavish cities, to the sunshine islands'
Rolling trophy cabinets of waterlife
That wobble past in gardens never worked upon

But steeped in paradise. As much a part of you
As all the grinding out of knowledge,
And, I guess, a speck on what remains

Unstarted and unthought. I urge you on
As madly as the football team I died for
On the terraces of youth, and keep a watching

Brief on still. Not quite nostalgia but
The odd retention of a link, a wish
To be there when they finally arrive amidst

The cheers and back slapping, the all
That never was and never quite believed in
I determine to live out, this time, inside

Your different destiny. Your head turns fiercely
Skywards as you ride away, scorning who stand
Before you with their arms outraised.

The Train Accident, Cannon Street

A clutter like a child's room
Untidied – vehicles are parked
Haphazardly along the road.
Adjacent streets, with tape, are marked.

The service workers are at ease.
In small communities they stand.
Their hot drinks steam like funnelled ships
Voyaging to a distant land.

The station's trellis gates are closed
As if they guard a sacred place
Or vault, whatever, it is barred
To members of the human race.

A train smashed through the buffers, then,
(We understand) the middle car
Reared, bronco like, and those inside
Were rattled like sweets in a jar.

Imagine, if you can, the scene,
As bits of debris fell like rain,
Each piece on its pre-destined course
Landing and taking off again.

Transfixed, the office workers stare
As if, while lunching in the street,
Some meaning flashed across their lives
As sunlight on a field of wheat.

But now the police move people on.
(There are no images of pain).
They trudge past restaurants and shops.
So ends this story of a train.

Mrs Bonavia

"Playboy" or "The Sun" might have killed her for her breasts;
Lost on her because her sheer bulk took her
Past girlishness. She was happiest in cleaning clothes
That hung in a straight line past her waist, like drapes.

When I saw her in the hall, drunk on cleaning fluids,
She beamed and brushed aside my stuttering offers
To assist. I imagined her inside the maisonette,
Storming the ramparts, bearing down on wayward surfaces.

I assumed her love for him matched her vastness, even though
He used to tout his portliness outside for hours
In his Sunday best, like a religious zealot, while she
Lay low, too bronchial and afraid to publicise

Her meagre dictionary. I cursed the times
I exited and turned into his arms, wondered
If he ever noticed how the door step gleamed like bullion
And their rooms stank of roses or heaven.

The Night Porter

At the reception desk, he stood impressively,
A large, clean-shaven man, just like his "Dad".
They worked together nights, saluted me,
Told me "Take care", as if I were a lad.

Until the day he told me, "Had a marriage…
Got a little girl", he seemed a loner,
Innocent perhaps. "Don't see her much…"
They lived away from London, west somewhere.

So this was exile – a kettle, keys,
Handwritten names inside a giant book,
A social life of residents' complaints,
The old folk thanking him with sweets or cake.

He left. I'd meet him in the streets,
First with his father, then alone.
His hair just kept on growing, next
A beard he never trimmed. Like to a son,

He'd give the same advice, "Take care",
From a back street bench confessed:
"Had trouble, lately, with the nerves…
Been visiting the centre – yes it's helped".

Since then he never fails to greet,
A nod or two, at times a "Hello there".
His hair has stopped, his features are a guess.
No longer does he ask that I take care.

Geneva

Hams, salamis rise like sculptures of rough seas.
"Now I should like to offer you some figs",
Tante Engel announces, and conjures a plateful.
"You like figs", she asks fiercely.
Onkel Detmar sighs over the Swiss economy.
A crescent of silver hair
Falls across his forehead boyishly.

Freed, we explore the city.
Mountains protect Geneva like a circle of flames.
Moored dinghies jostle in their hundreds.
We find a small beach they forgot to mention,
Ideal for children – hour-glass sands,
Margins of water fenced for safety.
Our son paddles and doesn't want to leave.

Early morning, Detmar drives us to the airport,
The air, crisp and clear with a few clouds,
An orange hue above the mountains.
"Look, Mont Blanc", he points suddenly,
And we locate its small triangle, rising
Beyond the vastness of the local range,
Distant, superior, a rim like moonlight.

Wimereux

CRAZY GOLF

Shuttered houses, gardens as hard
As gravel pits. This street leads down
To the sea. I can already feel
The air dispersing my asthma.

This village is so sensible.
The people are polite and the cars don't
Drive too fast. The shops are in
One street and don't sell rubbishy goods.

Today, we may play crazy golf.
There are wooden signs at the junctions
Tempting us – neatly carved arrows
With proper tips and tails.

CRABS

Among the rock pools we searched for crabs,
Turning over the larger rocks
With our hands. Whoever saw one first
Would shout so the others would not
Miss out on that scuttling,
Rubbery creature.

They were difficult to spot
In the fog-like storms
Out labour caused. Sand coloured crabs.
Most were pathetic or dead.
Nothing grand or regal
About Wimereux's crab population.

A PLAYGROUND CLOCK

I was waiting for you under the playground clock.
You were asleep with our son back at the hotel.
Children performed cartwheels in the sand,
Which was full of shadows – houses, contraptions…

Such a simple clock – straightforward hands and numbering,
An edging of blue. Unglamorous loos
In the white-washed building underneath.
But it told the right time, or near enough.

Sleep as long as you wish! For my part
I won't stray too far from my excellent clock.
The sea front is still warm and lively
And the cafes serve chocolate medallions with the café-au-lait!

PIRATES

They were sailing an inflatable dinghy
On the high seas.
You wanted to come aboard
Like a pirate with a dagger
Between his teeth.

But you were repelled
And the tears gushed down
Your once proud little pirate cheeks.
No more castles in the sand.
No more crab hunts.

We told you they were being mean,
And, instantly,
Your sobbing stopped.
Back across the sands you ran
And attacked them with spittle!

THE SEA-CAT

The Sea-Cat trundles out
Of Boulogne harbour
And curves across the seascape
As relaxed as a man smoking his pipe.

Strange how distance conceals
The rough and tumble
Of the Channel and gives us
This gentle vessel

Gliding beneath the horizon
Back to England,
Deceptively spick and span
In the sunlight.

A LITTLE PILE OF STUFF

I was the mover
Of our little pile
Of stuff as we scavenged
The beach, the camera,
Soggy, sand spattered
Shoes, groaning
paperbacks, a plastic
Windmill on a stick.

I kept glancing
Back to check
If anything had dropped,
Fearing the softness
of the sand might
Deaden its fall.

Christmas Lunch

The credentials of the Bonvias plummeted like shares.
'They never did write' said my friend,
Shampooing his car and brooding over an era's end.

They had returned to their roots like migrating birds.
'Came twice for Christmas lunch' he adjudged,
Measuring his words like stepping stones or a row of beads.

A sea dog of a face – tufted beard, swallow-like moustache.
His car shone like a capsule of sunlight.
'She done me proud' he insisted, as well he might.

SPORT, LOVE AND MISCELLANEOUS

Up the Blues

Almost a quarter of a century since we won the Cup.
Too many seasons we've dieted on salads served
On patios and sparkling like fragments of glass.
How we could do with one more juicy rump
To stab our forks into and make the blood erupt.

'Come on you Blues'. 'Go home you Liverpool'.
But the finished product all looks just a bit
Tip-toey through the tulips. There isn't anyone
To make a hunchback of the net from thirty yards.
Too many pretty boys. Too many flicks and chips.

But it's always, 'We'll support you evermore',
Not from the terraces, but from across the hills.
Years since I made the turnstiles click
Their tongues and turn like water mills.
But I love the teleprinter beeping me three points.

Cricket Helmets

They are handsome structures,
Like perfect igloos,
To defend the cranium,

Or, more complex in design,
With bars and vizors
Caging all the features.

Walking back, the occupants
Use them as bins for
Their gout-ridden gloves.

Snooker Players

They dip their cues across the baize, like angling,
Or using geiger counters in a search for minerals.
They line up shots like squinting through a hole.
They cue with the sudden thrusting of harpooning fish.

Immaculately styled hair and tailored evening wear.
Shoes gleam, unnaturally, as if electrically charged.
They progress around the table like hungry lions.
A scratch, scratch scratching as the tip is chalked.

In cubicles, they concentrate on cue and hands,
Using a cloth, like they were working to the bone.
They fuss about the balls, and will not play
Until convinced of surfaces as pure as molecules.

'*I am Your Travelling Supporter…*'

I am your travelling supporter. Do not be taken in
By the plain clothes and the pianissimo.
On the terraces, I rarely pinned
A pleated moon to my lapel or brandished,
Above my head, a clattering gate.

But I died for my team, just like all
The costumed balladeers. Were I a sea shell
You could press me to your ear and listen
To the inward ongoing roar
Crave your fulfillment as I craved the FA Cup.

Never think I might defect, and join the ones
Who stand in front of you with outraised arms
Like statues put there by a mischievous god.
These are no mighty megaliths.
One gust will hurtle them into the race of leaves.

'We Thank You For Submitting The Enclosed Bu
Regret We Are Unable To Make Use Of It.'

Sir,
We did not enjoy reading your poems.
We have no regrets about returning them.
We respectfully request that you do not send us any more.

Sir,
We publish only the best.
We discourage all beginners.
We are not interested in poets of 'promise'.

Sir,
Your work is shoddy and skirts round its subject.
Your self-expression is poor.
The clever metaphor fools us not.

Sir,
You do not have what it takes.
Give up ideas of joining the elite.
Please leave our hard-worked editors in peace.

Finally, sir,
May we interest you in a subscription?

Paul's Mini Market

It was a land where Gazza was king and Tottenham
A garden of earthly delights.
Business over, I indulged his whims and dreams.

His small TV flickered from a plank
Big Brother height above the drinks refrigerator.
After scores of Strongbow he was chanting my first name.

When I told him we were expecting a happy event,
He shook my hand, as if I had solved a difficult koan
Or won a scholarship into the rest of my life.

He took his family off to holiday in Canada,
And never came back. Later we heard he'd sold the lease.
Mountains 1 Spurs 0. He never saw our baby son.

The Bicycle Pump

You dragged your bike up the path.
Standing at the porch,
I thought I saw something fall.

After you had gone I discovered
Your pump, low down
On land behind the shallow wall.

I had to plunge my arm to rescue it.
Cans lay squashed. Wine bottles
Cratered the earth.

A Blue Track Suit

You were proud of it. Your first.
You wore it to the shops.
I fell out of love with thick material
And blue and bagginess.

I had a notion wearing something else
Might make it right again.
I longed to see you in the skirt
We chose on Princes Street

The day snow fell on Edinburgh.
I'd think of days we planned,
Driving to anywhere, lost in hills,
Leaving your blue track suit far behind.

A Harrap Columbus Coffee Mug

It was a gift from work. The outside
Repeated the words "Harrap Columbus".
The inside had the quality of marble.

I worked hard to keep it spotless,
Even the awkward parts around the base
Where I had to force the scourer.

But it wasn't long before familiar,
Stubborn bands appeared. Success
With coffee mugs had, again, eluded me.

Vigil

From the car's chill tomb I leaned, and looked
Towards the window, where I saw
The curtains closed and stereotyped. Ignored,
I turned away and, each few minutes, tried again,
But never saw the curtains flinch.

Were it not for the cold accumulating like wealth,
I might have stayed all night
Outside the house you were closeted inside,
Listening, discreetly, for the sound
Of an engine stammering like a fool.

In the end I worried I might fall ill,
So I drove away to find warmth,
Drove away between the comatosed houses,
Vowing goodness knows how many things,
Wondering if you would sleep that night better than I.

Vanishing

All those times
Our worlds failed
To connect,

You would take
To the streets,
Vanish into the darkness.

Sometimes I would follow,
Glimpse you beneath
A street light,

Striding, striding.
I could never explain

The throb of excitement
In my heart.

The Bedroom Poem

Patient, the bedroom waits for love.
Hot day, the window open wide.
In the slight breeze, the curtains move.

So solemnly, the wardrobe stands.
Clothes on the floor or draped on chairs.
A thirsty dressing-table plant.

What else than this could be more still?
When you will come I cannot tell.
Just that you will, just that you will.

A Bus Route at Night

At first we were always out there
In the cold nights, on the bus route lined
With dingy takeaways and sad hotels.
At times it seemed like another planet.

Once you cried after me. Your long coat
Hung from you as straight and wretchedly
As any down and out's, turning the food shops'
Galleries of flowers and spheres

Into a fairground glitter. When you ran
Towards me, you hurled aside the road
Like an old door wrenched from its hinges.
But happiness did not return that night.

Lighting Up

Outside my city offices
A garden flourishes;
Nestling against the building
Like a sleeping cat.

Fed up with my work I stare
At the garden from my desk.
When darkness falls, lights
On the railings tremble on.

Drinks

Here, on the fourth floor,
The vending machine works
Harder than I do.

Bookshop

So much on the shelves.
For months I have read
Not a single book.

A Cheque Guarantee Card

Arriving without honest money, I offer the glossed card,
Puzzled why he still, unflaggingly, accepts it.
Thus we consolidate a ritual, darken its roots.

Hundreds scurry onto his balance sheet like schools of fish.
In the half light, beside the stifled till,
He squints at numbers on the card's faint braille,

Writes and hands it back to me as if it were a bone
Stripped of its choicest meat. 'Can you manage' he enquires?
I cradle the goods, awkwardly, banish his concern.

FATHERHOOD

Your Face...

Your face is a round, laughing tragedy
Waiting to occur – a Chernobyl
Of the playroom, sealed, about to blow.

I watched you arrive, hoisted by the midwife
Above a crimson lake. You struggled,
As she held you, like a caught fish.

You gave birth to a contingent sorrow,
Something not on the balance sheet,
The consequences difficult to rehearse.

At sixteen months, I watch you rock
From toy to toy, placing them determinedly.
You chatter and bring me gifts.

Son Rising

6am. Over the bars
Of your cot your face
Rises like the sun.

Sunday

Golden flowers on the track,
But no trains.
I hold my son's hand.

Transitory

Your old-fashioned lampshade peers into the street
Like a one-eyed monster. In the summer months
The bulb is never lit, and I cannot tell if you are there,
Helter-skeltering between your commitments and your chores.

You had us mystified, the way you sometimes slowed
Into our lives, then throttled out again.
I often wondered how it would resolve.
The washing lines of cards, that hung

At Christmas from your ceiling, evidenced
Demands upon your time, and old disputes
Stayed close like watchful parents.
Near the end you took our baby son for walks,

Unprompted, and gave him two small story books –
Exquisite miniatures about a naughty cat.
I marvelled as you wheeled him like an old pro,
Taking the corners briskly, slalom style...

Piglets

We carry you to the end of the long garden
Where ten young piglets romp with mummy
In the mud. 'They've come to say hello' we tell you,
And they line up, curiously, like runners,
Jostling and champing at the bit.
They snort at us and we, in unison, snort back.

"I Buy My Dad..."

I buy my dad whatever toys he wants,
Dump trucks, diggers, dinosaurs
With fearsome teeth, mediaeval knights
And soldiers stuck to sentry boxes,
Puzzles, panda cars and fire engines
Whose ladders reach the sky.
We see them in shop windows on our walks.
"Would you like some of those?" I ask dad.
"Yes" he replies, "Yes, please".
So in we go and out we come with another
New toy. He's a pushover, my dad.

Bar Football

Alex plays
By his own rules
Which, at 4½,
Is just permissible.
"Mummy, I have to win"
He informs Mummy
Who gives up asking
If he wants to be
The blue team or
The red. A chunk of
Spending disappears
In favour of
A twelve ball
Footballing bonanza.
Mummy mustn't play
As Alex spots
Each ball precisely
At the feet of
Blue or red, then
Scuttles round
The table to locate
The handle that
Will flip the
Goal. Sometimes Mummy
Utters, "Goal, well
Played", her voice
Not quite as
Sprightly as
The words, her eyes
Adrift amongst
The bar's more adult
Games of
Coupling and
Flashing fruit.

I've drawn the
Longer straw,
Spectating,
Marvelling how
My son achieves
This latest
Cheat. Game over,
He returns
To mountaineer
A chair and tell me
In his cutely
Breathless way, "Daddy,
I won". Behind him
Trails the loser,
Sighing wonderfully.

Moon

How curious the moon is.
Sometimes it's a ball.
Sometimes there's not much of it,
Sometimes none at all.

But curiouser still is when
I'm told that I should say,
'Goodnight, moon, I'm off
To bed'. Cutely, I obey.

Teddy

'You're a tired boy' I tell you,
But you shake your head.
'Wouldn't you like to go up
With Teddy to bed?'

'You're a sleepy boy' I tell you,
'Teddy's sleepy too'.
So upstairs we all go –
Me, Teddy and you.